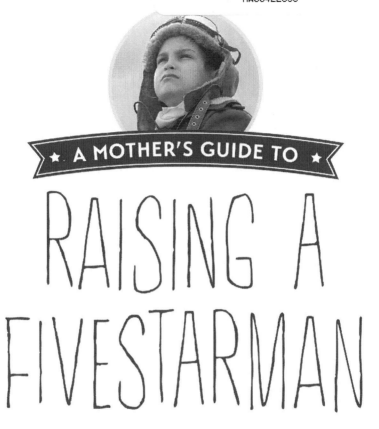

A MOTHER'S GUIDE TO

RAISING A FIVESTARMAN

★★★★★

by Neil Kennedy

A Mother's Guide to Raising a FivestarMan

DEDICATION

I want to dedicate this book to Kay, my wife and mother of my children. She has raised a FivestarMan, our son Chase, and two godly young women. Chase is so blessed because of the tremendous influence of his mother. Kay is an amazing woman of faith. She has a distinctive ear to hear God's Spirit regarding her children. She loves without measure and has genuinely supported our children in their dreams. I love you Kay Kennedy.

PROLOGUE

It's the end of another long day. Her body is exhausted. Her emotions are on edge. She can't imagine things ever getting better. The night has closed in on her. Laundry is a never-ending cycle, never satisfied, never caught up. The house barely resembles the home it once was. She hesitates as she lays her head on the pillow. She knows that the moment she does, the loneliness will set in—and it does—like a wave of oppression. She feels completely and utterly alone.

As she sleeps, she hears the whisper of a voice. She struggles to awaken, but the sleep is so heavy upon her she fights to unclench her eyes. The whisper is a prayer.

Her son is praying. She strains to hear his words.

> *"God, I need you to hear me. I need you to speak to me. My dad is gone. He's left my mommy. He's left... me. I don't know what to do. Who is going to teach me to play ball? Who is going to help me know what to do and how to do it? How am I going to become a man? Oh, God, help me. Help me to become a man—a real man. If you will, I will serve you. I will care for my mother."*

Her eyes, as clenched as they are, drip tears. The tears run down her face and dampen her pillow. She utters her own soft prayer, *"Please, God, help me raise my son to be a man."*

INTRODUCTION

I didn't have a father to raise me. Yes, my mother remarried after my parents divorced, but her husband was not a father to me. We occupied the same home, but he didn't mentor me. I wish I could express some gratitude for his provision; frankly, the deficits completely outweigh any addition that he might have brought.

Even as a boy, as naïve as I was, I still had a goal that motivated me concerning the kind of man I wanted to be. It was simple. I had a deep desire to be the kind of man I always wanted my mother to be married to. I desperately wished to become the kind of father that I wanted to have in my own life.

As simplistic as that sounds, it was motivating. The problem was that I didn't know how to become that kind of man. I didn't know what an authentic man was, much less how to be one.

Now, closing in on three decades of marriage and having three grown children, that simple goal has brought me to lead the charge on a national movement to resurrect authentic manhood, called FivestarMan.

WHAT IS A FIVESTARMAN?

He's the prince of every fairy tale. He's the hero of every movie. He's the model of the man every woman wants to marry and the fulfillment of every mother's dream for her son.

The principles that make a FivestarMan come from the foundational precept of Proverbs 20:5 which says, *"The purposes of a man's heart are deep waters, a man of understanding draws them out."*

The Hebrew word translated as *"man"* is *"iysh."* This word is specifically speaking to the masculine male, as opposed to a woman. The Hebrew word *"iysh,"* or *"man"* in the passage in Proverbs 20:5, encompasses five characteristics of defined purpose for an authentic man. These divinely ordained purposes for man are for him to be:

- **Adventurous**
- **Entrepreneurial**
- **Gallant**
- **Faithful**
- **Philanthropic**

When your son gains understanding of these five purposes that lie within him, his life will become a passionate pursuit of authentic manhood.

I have known what it is to struggle with defined purposes. I experienced the embarrassment of not knowing who I was. I felt as if the whole world was on a pace that I wasn't on—I couldn't catch up. I wanted to reach and grasp understanding, but it eluded me.

Ma'am, I do not know your situation.

You may be the wife of a FivestarMan who takes care of your family and leads your home in a godly manner. Or you may be a widow or single mother, raising your child alone without a strong male role model to look to.

Or you may fall somewhere in between.

Whatever your situation, my heart goes out to you. It is a formidable calling to endeavor to raise up a man of God in this day and age. If you are a single parent, married to an unbeliever, or a mother without a godly male influence in your son's life, I can't imagine the pain that is in your heart knowing your son may be experiencing the kind of struggle I went through as a young boy. I want to help. That's why I am writing this book for you.

Whether you are married to a wonderful man, or are currently battling through the worst of family circumstances, I want to equip you with an understanding of what an authentic man is designed to be. I want to show you God's original intent for creating your son.

My prayer is that you will be encouraged and receive confidence and hope that your son will grow into the man you desire for him to become.

Along with this guidebook, please get your son a copy of **FivestarMan—The Five Passions of Authentic Manhood** and a copy of the **FivestarMan 45-Day Challenge and Field-Guide.** I know it will help him as you work to guide him into becoming the man that God has purposed for him to be.

—Neil Kennedy

TABLE OF CONTENTS

CHAPTER ONE
RAISE A DIRTY BOY

Within every boy is a spirit of adventure. There is something about the field that calls to a boy. It may be a football field, a baseball field, a soccer field, and yes, even a battlefield. It's on the field of contest where a boy relates to other boys. This may not set well with a woman's personal sensitivities, but men relate to each other differently than women do.

Solomon said, *"As iron sharpens iron, so one man sharpens another"* (Proverbs 27:17 NIV).

As a boy faces the challenge of competition, he becomes stronger, faster and smarter. The field of contest makes him better.

This is something that you may struggle with, but I promise you, you must allow your son to get out on the field and get dirty. That's right. You must raise a dirty boy.

As tempting as it is, you must resist the urge to raise your son in a perfectly safe and sterile environment. The adventurous spirit that resides within your son is a deposit of purpose that will come into play later in his life. If you don't allow him to gain understanding of his adventurous nature, you may distort his character and frustrate his personality.

The Adventurous Spirit helps a boy embrace the concepts of risk and reward. The misunderstanding of risk and reward has weakened our culture's understanding of this primal motivation. Our politically correct society demands that every participant gets a trophy; however, when every boy gets a trophy, no trophy has meaning.

I get it. I understand that a lot of mothers don't want their sons' feelings to be hurt. But if you shelter your son from facing the pain of defeat, you will also exclude him from the thrill of victory. Doing so will take away one of the most powerful tools that lies within a man—the desire to compete and win.

You will do more harm to his competitive nature than anything else if you don't allow your son to experience both winning and losing.

It's not easy to watch your child suffer the pain of a loss, but it will help him in the long run. Sports are life's metaphor. A sheltered child will face a harsh reality if he always receives accolades and never experiences loss while growing up. The real world of business is not so kind. There are always distinct winners and losers.

Not every boy wants to play football, basketball, baseball or soccer, but every boy needs some type of field to conquer.

THE FIELD OR THE FANTASY

Some mothers are so fearful that their sons may get hurt in the great outdoors that, as an alternative, they encourage their sons to stay inside and simply play video games.

God has a bigger plan for your son than sitting on the couch playing fantasy games with his joystick. Don't allow your son to limit his competition to the realm of imagination. He needs to relate to other boys on a field of competition. His adventurous nature needs to feel the earth underneath him.

There is an important warning in the scriptures that concerns vain imaginations.

> ...They became futile and godless in their thinking
> [with vain imaginings, foolish reasoning, and stupid
> speculations] and their senseless minds were darkened.
> Claiming to be wise, they became fools [professing to
> be smart, they made simpletons of themselves].
> Romans 1:21-22 AMP

I believe you must be careful not to allow your son to spend all his time playing imaginary games. It leads to uncontrolled vain imaginations and desensitizes him to reality.

According to a study in 2010, the Kaiser Family Foundation reported that the average teen spends fifty hours per week in front of a screen (computer, television, gaming). That's a full-time job plus ten hours of overtime!

It's hard to imagine what the repercussions will be on these teenagers who devote so much of their life experience to a fantasy world. In the future, we will face delusional young men who can't tell the difference between reality and their imaginations.

Another danger of the over-hyped fantasy world is that it produces social ineptitude. Your son cannot develop proper relationships with people in the real world, if his understanding of connections is only with fantasy characters.

"Adventure, with all its requisite danger and wildness, is a deeply spiritual longing written into the soul of man." —John Eldredge

There is something very spiritual about a boy experiencing nature. Getting out in the field of God's creation can provide deeply spiritual moments.

Throughout Scripture, men related to God in the field. Adam related in the Garden; Noah on the waters; Abraham in a new territory; Moses on a mountain; King David in a shepherd's pasture; and when Jesus spent His time on the earth, He withdrew into the wilderness.

Boys love to hunt, fish or hike in the wilderness. It's important for them to feel the wildness of the field.

THE TWINS OF CONTENTION

Your son has two natures.

The Bible gives us some insight on two boys who were raised in the same household yet were opposites in nature. Isaac and Rebekah had twins. I call them the twins of contention. It seems that a boy often wrestles with two natures within him. Esau represents one, and Jacob represents the other.

Esau, which means *"red,"* was so named because he was born covered with red hair. Jacob was named *"deceiver,"* because he clutched the heel of his brother, grasping for the status of being first born.

Esau became a hunter, a man of the field, and he loved wild game. His father spent most of his time with him. Isaac loved Esau; however, Esau wasn't balanced in his approach to life. He spent all of his time in the field. Esau wasn't a thinker. His whole life was about the field of contest.

Some boys grow up and all they have on their mind is going fishing, hunting or sports. Although I do highly recommend that your boy should sharpen his skills on the field of contest, it should be his hobby, not his whole life.

On the other hand, Jacob was a momma's boy. He was always close to the tents. He learned to cook. His mother, Rebekah, taught her son the tricks of manipulation and deceit.

Jacob allowed his thinking to become vanity. He thought only about himself. He struggled with the insecurity of being the younger brother. He resented Esau's flippant attitude toward the birthright. Jacob coveted what he could never rightfully have, even grasping the heel of his brother for it at birth. These twins of contention wrestled in the womb and later grappled in life.

Jacob took advantage of his weakened brother by deception, and Esau was foolish enough to exchange his birthright for a bowl of soup. Jacob's act of manipulation proved to be a snare between the brothers. Using the deceptive skills of his mother,

Jacob received the blessing from his father in the place of his elder brother. Then later as retribution, Jacob suffered the consequences of the skills of manipulation from his father-in-law, Laban.

Here's my point: If you don't allow your son to have a balanced approach between the field and the tent, you may raise a son who doesn't value the things that are truly important, or he may rely upon manipulation and deception to get his way.

In the end, Esau lived a life with bitter morsels toward his brother's ambition, and Jacob lived a life deceiving and being deceived.

GOD WRESTLES WITH YOUR BOY ALONE

> *And Jacob was left alone, and a Man wrestled with him until daybreak.*
>
> *Genesis 32:24 AMP*

God will deal with your son, but He will do it when he is alone.

This may be one of the most difficult things a mother must face, the idea that she must allow her son to wrestle with God alone, yet it is in the moments of isolation where he will find the fight of a man.

God won't deal with your son in a group setting. It will be in a moment of isolation. God wrestles one on one.

This is not a hard and fast rule, but typically, I have found that around the age of twelve, a boy begins to have a stirring passion in his heart concerning God. This may seem a little young to some, but it was certainly true in my case.

When I was twelve years of age, I awakened to a realization that God wanted to begin to speak to me. I didn't know how to explain it to anyone around me, so I begin to have a quiet dialogue with God.

My sport of choice was wrestling. It seemed as if I often wrestled with God. This is when I shook off vanity and trivial ideologies and got into the grasp of Someone stronger and more powerful than I could ever dream. I found myself wrestling with Someone who wanted to make me stronger and train me to be a better man than even I wanted to be.

Proverbs says, *"Wounds from a friend can be trusted"* (Proverbs 27:6 NIV). God grappled with me. He pushed me. He challenged me.

Every move I tried on Him, He countered with a more strategic blow. It was simply awesome. I found the intimacy of the fight. I discovered the blessing of wrestling with God.

Jacob said, *"I will not let you go unless you bless me"* (Genesis 32:26 NIV).

A boy desires his father's blessing. It is a deep need in every young man. Jacob used deception to get his earthly father's blessing and was grasping at the Angel of the Lord to get his spiritual Father's blessing.

Your son's father may or may not be in his life. No matter what your situation, God will deal with your son personally. God will wrestle with him alone. You may notice this becoming more intense, beginning around the time when he is twelve years of age.

This will be a very special time for both of you. You will need discernment while he is experiencing this personal and intimate relationship with God. Ask God for insight and understanding so that you will not infringe upon the process.

YOUR SON MUST BE PREPARED

Every boy sees a field differently. Some see it as a place to throw and catch a ball. Others see a place to ride motocross or bicycles. Others want to hunt or hike the trails. It is the field where boys experience adventure.

David was born the eighth child of Jesse. He was small and ruddy, good looking in a boyish way. He was loyal and truthful. Being the youngest, he was tasked with the lower-level position of shepherding the sheep. He was in the pasture many times alone, isolated, left to practice his slingshot, or ponder the stars at night.

Isolation is a unique experience.

After graduating high school, I was hired at strip coalmine to pump water seven nights a week, from 7:00 p.m. to 7:00 a.m. I was young, naïve and hungry. I needed work, and it was good pay. I worked alone.

You can imagine the isolation that I felt. The coalmine was in a rural area of Oklahoma. I worked in an open pit about 80 to 100 feet below ground level. It was dangerous work.

Solomon said, *"The laborer's appetite works for him; his hunger drives him on"* (Proverbs 16:26 NIV).

I look back now, and as difficult as those nights were, I realize they were the conditioning of my life. Those nights of isolation became my pasture of preparation.

My mind was occupied with the thought, *What am I going to do in life?* That thought became a prayer, and then God began to speak with me in the pasture.

There may come a time when your son withdraws—it may be to his room or into a field, but he may withdraw to have intimate conversation with his Father, his God.

Jesus withdrew often into the wilderness or the lake. He spent an amazing amount of time away from people.

The lessons that your son can learn in isolation will be life changing:

> **Isolation is intimidating.**
> It is a place where he will discover vulnerabilities. It will expose his weaknesses, fears, and insecurities.
>
> **Isolation is quiet.**
> The clutter of noise is quieted when a boy is isolated, and his spirit begins to speak louder.
>
> **Isolation is revealing.**
> Your son will discover there is much activity happening around him, much of which he was previously unaware. Isolation will help him notice what others overlook.

Isolation will expand him.
When a young man is always with the crowd, the
crowd begins to place their limitations on him. When
he stands alone, maybe under the stars, the outer
limits begin to be accessible. No one ever thought
of going to the moon without first looking at it and
saying, "Why not?"

Isolation will test his character.
It will help him determine who he is and who he can
become. His character will be forged in the secret
place between him and God.

INDIVIDUALITY

Some boys are raised with the idea they must do something
outrageous or grand to be noticed in life. Our pop culture
models this as the fast track to fame.

The problem with this faux-fame is that it produces caricatures,
not character. In their attempt to be noticed, young men begin
to adopt artificial mannerisms. They feel the need to pierce
or tattoo their bodies in attempts to make a mark on their
surroundings. Their body markings are their attempt to be
different; yet, they only demonstrate their loss of individuality.

Don't get me wrong; I am not an old-fogey who thinks this is
the unpardonable sin. The problem is, young men are marking
themselves at the age of naïveté, and most likely will regret it
later. Some will find their pierced ears, spaced ears, or pinned
tongues, lips, eyebrows, and noses will limit their opportunities.
Few higher-wage jobs will be available to someone who doesn't
"look the part."

Tattoos and piercings have their roots in paganism and hedonism. I realize that this practice has taken on a less spiritual root today; however, it is very important that we're not flippant about the motivation behind it.

The Bible speaks of the prophets of Baal who cut themselves and marked their bodies, crying out to a god who could not hear them. Unfortunately, we have a generation that is desperately crying out to fathers who are not listening.

Most who are marking themselves are not doing it to be different; they are doing it to be heard.

Your son must realize his contribution to the world will not come from copycat strategies but from digging deep into God's original intent for him. This revelation doesn't come easily. It comes from seeking, knocking and asking what God will open up to him.

Your son will not be authentic to his manhood if he simply copies what he sees someone else doing. The revelation of true individuality comes from the inner stream of insight that only his spirit reveals (1 Corinthians 2:11). Those who copy the crowd become distorted caricatures of others rather than developing their own character.

Jesus forged His individuality when he went into isolation without food and water for forty days and nights. He had to battle strange voices that attempted to alter his destiny. But after Jesus emerged from the wilderness experience, He knew who He was and what He was called to accomplish.

This experience gave Jesus the confidence He would need to face the constant schemes of His enemies and the questioning of the world that would come.

"Nothing of great value is ever achieved without facing violent opposition." —Albert Einstein

---

Once again, the field of contest is a training camp of life. It is a metaphor for overcoming obstacles, opposition and objections.

THE TENT OF TRAINING

Your son needs to be an apprentice.

As valuable as isolation is to developing individuality, your son also needs a time of training.

Wisdom is either gained through experiences of pain or through mentors. I suggest mentors. Every young man needs a mentor.

Donald Trump's program, **The Apprentice** is a unique experience for those seeking to step into a new realm of business acumen. **The Apprentice** puts novice professionals under the leadership of a billionaire mogul to learn from him. Doing so makes them become better equipped to take on the business world.

You should cultivate in your son an appetite to read biographies of great men. I know that there are great women who model wisdom; however, your son needs to see real men facing the challenges of life. (Remember, we're talking about raising a FivestarMan.)

David, the young shepherd, had an artistic gift of strumming the harp (a modern instrument would be a guitar), writing and singing songs.

> *A man's gift maketh room for him, and bringeth him*
> *before great men.*
>
> Proverbs 18:16

David's preparation met with opportunity. The delusional and tormented King Saul needed soothing music to help bring peace into his atmosphere, so his advisors called for young David to use his musical skills and prophetic psalms to comfort the king.

Every opportunity to be mentored is an opportunity to learn— from both wisdom and foolishness. While serving the king, David was able to observe the king's way of doing business, making decisions both good and bad, and seeing the protocols that were required to petition the king. This would prove invaluable later, when David would fulfill his individual destiny as the King of Israel.

Look for opportunities for your son to be mentored in work. Be careful and choose mentors wisely. They will have a profound influence on your son and should not be allowed to overreach into your son's life. (In chapter three, I will talk about who your son should call, "Daddy," or "Father." This is an important warning to hear.)

Please note that mentors are not replacements for fathers.

Most of my mentors in life never knew me. I read their stories or watched them from afar. Some of my mentors, once I got to know them, lost their influence upon my life because I stumbled over their humanity. Their gift to me was lost.

This is an important point to mention: Mentors are not perfect. They are simply men who have perfected an area of interest that your son can learn from.

YOUR SON NEEDS A COACH

Solomon said, *"If the axe is dull... more strength is needed"* (Ecclesiastes 10:10 NIV).

It's important that your son has and maintains a learning attitude. Before he jumps into something, invest in some training. You should both do your homework on the subject and find out what you need to know. This will save your son some embarrassment and give him confidence to take on an endeavor.

I remember when I was about twelve, and I wanted to start wrestling. My mom was busy working, and I really didn't know how to approach her on the subject, so I just showed up one day at practice. I didn't have the equipment, the workout gear or the shoes. I just showed up. It was embarrassing when I told the coach, "I want to wrestle, but I don't know anything about it." Unfortunately, he didn't help much. I practiced the first few days in street clothes until I realized what I needed to bring. After practice, I walked the five or six miles home for many days before my mother even realized that I wasn't riding the bus.

If we could have done our homework and investigated what I needed to wear, what was expected of me, and how we could manage the practices, it would have helped me to have a better start in a sport that I grew to love.

David sharpened his skill by seeing and hearing King Saul make decisions. Unaware of his protégé, Saul didn't know that the heir to his throne was sitting in the room.

*"Unless you've been faithful to another man's
possession, you are not qualified to manage your own."*
Luke 16:12 Author's Paraphrase

Every young man needs to learn from a coach. A champion is simply an average young man in whom a coach saw potential and drew it out.

THE BALCONY OF BOREDOM

The greatest challenge your son will battle is boredom.

David won every battle on the field of contest, except the one on the balcony of boredom.

The Bible tells of a disastrous decision David made based on the counsel of his advisors. At the time when kings went out to war, David stayed at home (1Chronicles 20:1).

> *One evening David got up from his bed and walked
> around on the roof of the palace. From the roof he saw
> a woman bathing. The woman was very beautiful, and
> David sent to find out about her....*
> *2 Samuel 11:2-3 NIV*

It is very important that you do not allow your son to be bored. He needs to be active. Make sure that his day is full and that he manages his energy by spending it on healthy activity. Loss in the battle with boredom leads a boy to temptation.

(I will talk more about relationships with women in chapter three, "He Wants To Be The Hero.")

GET PRACTICAL

- Develop an exercise program for your son.
- Discover a sport that your son enjoys.
- Look for opportunities for your son to go hunting, fishing, hiking, etc.
- Push your son out of his room and into the field in some capacity.
- Look for camps or weekend events that force him to be active.

The bottom line is that your son needs to get dirty. He needs to gain some scrapes and bruises. He may get hurt and even feel some pain, but that will be a better character-building experience than sitting in apathy on the couch, bored with life, and insecure about his future.

A young FivestarMan must experience the field of contest!

Chapter Two
MAKE YOUR SON A MONEY MAGNET

The very first words God spoke over man were a blessing, *"Be fruitful and increase"* (Genesis 1:28 NIV).

This theme of increase is echoed throughout the Scriptures. God not only blessed Adam, He repeated the blessing upon Noah and his sons. Then thousands of years later, Jesus spoke it over His disciples.

Your son is created in the shadowed image of God (Genesis 1:27). I know this is a powerful statement, but it's true. Man is designed to recreate after his own kind—to increase. Your position as a mother is powerful in that you begin to lay the foundation for your son's understanding of increase.

It is vitally important for a young man to comprehend that he is designed for increase. Increase is in his DNA; his genetic code dictates to every fiber of his being to increase.

You will find this principle counter cultural. Today we are battling an anti-man spirit. The propaganda of our time is a constant barrage of anti-human expansion. Population control—by abortion, euthanasia, or genocide—is the agenda of many elite theorists who have seized control of higher learning institutions, governments and other organizations around the world. This agenda is based upon a lie of popular economics, which states that the world contains a limited supply of physical resources (land, oil, gas, minerals, etc.), and wealth is determined by the control and management of those resources.

This premise as a foundational thought creates a chain reaction of erroneous pursuits. It demonstrates an amazing flaw in the thinking of secular man. This posturing places these theorists in direct opposition to the purpose of God and His original intent for man.

Man has a nemesis, a satanic spirit that works against his expansion upon the earth. This principality is constantly scheming against man's dominion of the earth. You see its prints on government, media, education, and cultural influences, and even on some religious institutions.

It is a covetous and hypocritical spirit that drives those who are presently living to argue against more people having the opportunity to live.

We believe in God. We believe in Intelligent Design, on purpose and for purpose. The characteristics of God are described this way: He is omnipotent (all powerful); He is omniscient (all knowing); and He is omnipresent (all present). God is also predestinate, which means He knew the end before the world began. With the character of God affirmed and unchangeable, we can be assured that God is wise enough to put more than enough resources within His creation to not only sustain the bare necessities of that creation, but also to give it abundance.

*Delight thyself also in the LORD: and he shall give thee
the desires of thine heart.*

Psalm 37:4

Your son needs to be raised with a deep understanding of his
purpose to increase; that's the entrepreneurial drive within him.

When I say he has an entrepreneurial purpose, I am stating that
your son has a divine deposit, a gift within him. If he gains a real
understanding of this, he will never want for his needs. He will
also fulfill the desires of his heart and finance his purpose.

That gift is called a vocation, which literally means a "divinely
spoken call." A vocation is what God has spoken over us; a
profession is what we speak over ourselves.

God has spoken over your son. Yes, your son has a divine
"word" spoken over him to give him purpose.

THE LAW OF EXCHANGE

This world operates on the Law of Exchange. Money is simply
the currency that represents the exchange.

Let me explain what I mean by that.

When a man receives money, he does so because someone else
believed what that man possessed—time, ability, or intellect—
was more valuable than the dollars that were in their hands.
They made an exchange.

When I was a young man, I didn't have proven abilities or a
track record of successes. Consequently my exchange rate was

minimal. As I was educated and developed skills; however, my exchange rate grew exponentially.

We live in a society that seems to want everyone to have a minimal existence—no one should have too much or too little. But this belief system destroys the motivational influence of the entrepreneurial drive and causes people to develop a maintenance mentality. You must resist this kind of average thinking if you want the best for your son.

Jesus gave an example of this when He told the story of a businessman who, when preparing for an excursion, entrusted his money to three different managers. The entrepreneur assigned his portfolio to his management team according to their proven abilities. After a season of time, the owner returned to conduct an audit. The first manager doubled the owner's wealth, as did the second manager. The third manager maintained the sum entrusted to him, but he did not generate any increase.

The entrepreneur's response was an enlightened glimpse into the character of God. The owner responded with generosity toward the first two managers, but the third manager, the one who merely maintained the wealth, was terminated. He was fired!

Your son has more potential in him than maintenance. He is destined for more than mediocrity. As a mother, you can help him draw upon the entrepreneurial drive within him to give him the life he desires.

Abraham was a great model of a biblical entrepreneur. He had to leave his father's household in order to fulfill his destiny. God told him, *"Leave your country, your people and your father's household and go to the land I will show you"* (Genesis 12:1).

Abraham received his directions from God, even though he didn't know where he was being led. This is an example of remarkable faith.

God's instruction was very precise. He said, *"Go to the land I will show you and it will be your inheritance."* (See Genesis 12:1-7.)

Abraham was the first person recorded to use land as a commodity to own and to exchange. He discussed the price of his property, defined its boundaries by legal description, and made the transaction a public notice to be honored down through the generations. This is the foundation for real estate transactions even until today.

Solomon said, *"He who works his land will have abundant food, but the one who chases fantasies will have his fill of poverty"* (Proverbs 28:19 NIV).

There is an important lesson in this verse; the person who establishes his wealth through work will experience abundance. Once again, a fantasy chaser will only have poverty.

Teach your son to establish himself. Teach him to take steps that are ordered, directional and intentional. Teach your son to work.

Some men become nomadic in their employment. They are constantly chasing a dollar. But the only way to really gain wealth is by taking systematic steps toward a determined goal.

Abraham started as a nomad, wandering through the land of Canaan, until the Lord showed him the powerful truth of ownership. It was then that Abraham established himself with real property. In fact, the Bible says that he gained eight other sources of income, as well as his land—sheep, cattle, silver, gold, menservants, maidservants, camels and donkeys!

Solomon gives us insight that this is wisdom, *"Give a portion to seven, yes, even [divide it] to eight, for you know not what evil may come upon the earth"* (Ecclesiastes 11:2 AMP).

Abraham's example of entrepreneurship demonstrates that your son can become extremely wealthy if he can master the ownership and exchange of real and intellectual property.

Teach your son to observe what's hidden. There are multitudes of secrets yet to be revealed on the earth. He could be the man to discover them.

Let me give you a few examples.

Matt White was the first billionaire baseball player; however, he didn't make his money through baseball. He made it by helping out a family member in need. Matt was a struggling pitcher with the Los Angeles Dodgers when he purchased fifty acres of land from his aunt who needed to sell her property to move into a nursing home.

After the purchase, White hired a surveyor to inspect his land only to find that the land was solid Goshen stone, estimated to be worth over $2.5 billion.

Few people are wise enough to see beyond the obvious.

T. Boone Pickens is best known for his Pickens Energy Plan to wean the United States off of foreign oil dependence, but I like a part of his story that few people know.

Mr. Pickens purchased a ranch in Texas. Being a man who made his money by looking underneath the dirt, T. Boone had a survey done to look beneath his property. He discovered a huge reservoir of water that he tapped into. He signed leases with his neighbors and built a pipeline to the Dallas/Ft. Worth metropolitan area to supply them with water. His simple land survey became a billion dollar venture.

George Washington Carver, the great scientist, botanist and inventor, discovered how to tap into the hidden secrets of resource.

Burdened by the infestation of the boll weevil, the southern cotton fields were being destroyed. Mr. Carver walked through his laboratory, reached into a bin of peanuts, raised a handful toward heaven and prayed, "God, Creator of the universe, reveal to me the secrets which you have housed within the peanut."

This simple prayer led to hundreds of practical discoveries that turned the entire southern farming industry around.

The omniscient God designed your son after His own image with sustenance inside him. When God spoke to the land, He said, "Produce!" When God spoke to the seas, He said, "Teem with creatures!" When God spoke to Himself, He said, "Let us make man!"

Your son must know his Source! When he knows his Source, he will discover his potential.

It is absolutely vital that your son is exposed to the principle of the entrepreneurial drive. Having this base knowledge will empower him to passionately pursue and discover his God-given vocation.

GET PRACTICAL

- Look for opportunities for your son to attend seminars, simulcasts, and business events at community clubs such as the Chamber of Commerce.
- Resource your son with Dave Ramsey's book **Financial Peace for Children.** He has a great financial starting plan for students. (www.daveramsey.com)
- Teach your son basic skills such as developing an envelope system of cash management or maintaining a checking account.
- Have your son do household work and yard work for money rather than simply giving him money.
- Give your son a financial reward for reading books on business or money management. There are plenty of books written in a simple form.

You don't want your son living in systemic poverty, relying upon hand-me-downs and benevolence. You want the best for him, so strengthen his understanding that he determines his own economy.

As a FivestarMan, he has an entrepreneurial gift within him, a deposit of the Divine, a resource to meet his needs, satisfy his desires, and fulfill his purpose.

Chapter Three
HE WANTS TO BE THE HERO

The themes of the popular comics are pretty simple. The stories are very similar in rhythm. An enemy wants to destroy innocent lives and the hero with unusual, or even supernatural abilities, fights against the odds to win the day and save the victim from impending disaster. Every boy reading these stories sees himself as that conquering hero.

But somewhere in the daily grind, the thrill of life is dulled by the routine. The glamorous expectations of saving the world from destruction are lost in a boring existence of home, school and work.

Yet, deep inside your son lies a courageous, chivalrous and gallant purpose. Understanding this purpose will become a strong motivator in his management of relationships.

A FivestarMan is gallant. This means that he shows special attention and respect toward women in an honorable way. He treats women who are older than he as his own mother. He treats younger women as his own daughter or sister. He treats his peers with tremendous dignity and respect.

When your son gains understanding of this gallant purpose, it will draw upon one of the most amazing qualities that a man possesses, yet is rarely conditioned in modern culture: Honor.

Our society is suffering from a lack of honorable conduct. There was a time in American history when men would stand on riverbanks to duel for the sake of honor. That day has passed.

Growing up in Oklahoma, I was taught that fighting was appropriate only for the sake of defending your honor. The only fights I was ever involved in were over my honor or for the protection of a girl.

There is a dangerous mindset being adopted in our modern culture—it's the idea of appeasement. It is a cowardly approach to life and will result in men being dominated by ruthless and irrational ideologists.

There are times when capitulation is not the answer. We must be willing and able to defend our dignity (the dignity of being a man) and the honor of a woman.

HOW CAN YOU KEEP YOUR SON PURE?

American society lost the directional markers of purpose in the 1960s. The sexual revolution ushered in degradation in our culture. In fact, the very idea of remaining sexually pure is laughable to some; yet, it is gaining resurgence among the younger generation, especially among young men. This is a welcome backlash from the overexposure of sexual content in the media. Some young men are seeing the value of purity for themselves and are attracted to young women who have respected themselves enough to remain pure.

With so much sexual impurity in the world today, how can your son keep himself pure?

Solomon, a man who wrote most of the Book of Proverbs, gives your son guidance:

- Pay attention to wisdom (Proverbs 7:1-5).
- Don't give an ear to seductive words (Proverbs 7:5).
- Keep your distance from seductive women (Proverbs 7:6-8).
- Don't stray around her presence (Proverbs 7:9).
- Learn to bounce your eyes from gazing upon a woman (Proverbs 7:10-13).
- Understand the difference between lust and love (Proverbs 7:18).
- Know the boundaries of the relationship of marriage (Proverbs 7:19).
- Have the confidence to reject inappropriate advancements from women (Proverbs 7:21).
- Understand that impurity is a trap (Proverbs 7:22-23).
- Be forewarned that you will be embarrassed and destroyed by inappropriate relationships (Proverbs 7:23).

Keeping pure is not going to be easy for your son, but it is possible. There is a gallant and honorable purpose for doing so.

I know you want the best for your son. Few people get to experience the incredible rewards of a relationship that has endured through the years, with the layers and layers of intimacy that dig deep into the depths of a passionate love. You may not have even had that yourself, but your son can.

You son will be exposed to a barrage of sexually suggestive material. Unfortunately that is simply the case in today's day and age. You will not be able to filter out every show, Internet site, music genre, or friend who wants to introduce him to crude and inappropriate sexual content; however, you can teach your son how to treat a girl like a lady. Believe it or not, if he is a Christian, your son has within him a governing conscience of moral purity. If you will nurture that conscience, he can develop a dignity of discipline.

You may find that young women are aggressive in the pursuit of your son. This can be a real challenge. Ask God to give you discernment and wisdom in how to deal with it.

KEEP AN ATMOSPHERE OF PEACE IN YOUR HOME

Very few people realize the devastating effect strife has within the home. Strife is an extremely destructive environment. The Bible says that where there is strife, there is every kind of evil (James 3:16).

One of the gates you must guard is the gate that media flows through into your home. I know how difficult this can be, but you must realize that it is vitally important that you protect your son from the overwhelmingly destructive influence of this culture.

This won't be easy. You can't (and shouldn't) try to isolate your son from the world. That doesn't work in the long run but usually only causes an extreme attraction to it later, often causing a rebellion against every rule that you tried to use to isolate him. You must teach your son how to discern the difference between the truth of God and the lies of this world.

A balanced approach to music, television and movies is recommended. If you become too rigid, your son may rebel. If you are too permissive, your son may allow destructive appetites to flow freely into his life.

ATTEND A CHURCH THAT SUPPORTS PROPER RELATIONSHIPS

Your son needs a church that promotes the ideas of authentic manhood, a church that shows honor and respect toward women, and provides safe and spiritually maturing programs to help raise your son in the instruction of God's Word.

Some churches have an imbalanced approach toward women. A few have an overemphasis of women in leadership, while others misuse Scripture and masculine authority to oppress women.

Has the fruit of your pastor's teaching produced a healthy family in his own home? Does the leadership in your church model a strong family life?

You will need to discuss the Word of God with your son. I strongly recommend that you raise your son with the daily habit of reading the Book of Proverbs. Proverbs is a book of lessons from a man's perspective. There are 31 chapters in the Book of Proverbs—one chapter for each day of the month.

A good place to start developing this habit is for you to read passages from Proverbs to him while he is eating breakfast. Then ask him which one stood out to him the most, and discuss the meaning of it. The principles contained in these chapters are extremely powerful and will prove themselves invaluable in his life.

As he matures, continue to have him read a chapter of Proverbs each day. This should become a habit that sets in his rhythm of life. You will be amazed at the results.

Years ago, as a young pastor, I encouraged our teenagers in the church to read one chapter of Proverbs every day. I promised them that if they did, they would make straight As in all of their classes. That was a bold prediction; however, I felt comfortable making that guarantee because of chapter one. Proverbs 1 promises that those who read its passages will gain wisdom and discipline, understanding and prudence, knowledge and discretion.

Two of the teenagers took my challenge to heart, and four years later, both became the valedictorians of their two local high schools. I remember hearing the first one speak at his graduation, then rushing to the next one to hear the other boy's speech. I can't tell you how excited I was to see the results of this promise. Both boys acknowledged in their commencement speeches that reading Proverbs was pivotal in their success. By the way, they both received full academic scholarships to leading universities, saving their families tens of thousands of dollars.

When looking at the Scriptures, look for principles that your son can apply to his life. Boys want practical instruction and application.

THE FATHER'S HEART

Look, I am sending you the prophet Elijah before the great and dreadful day of the Lord arrives. His preaching will turn the hearts of fathers to their children, and the hearts of the children to their fathers. Otherwise, I will come and strike the land with a curse.

Malachi 4:5-6 NLT

There is no doubt that as a society, we are reaping a whirlwind of the destructive byproduct of absentee fatherhood. The statistics give overwhelming proof that as fathers have abandoned their responsibilities to raise up their children, their children are living under what seems to be a curse.

You may be in the difficult position of raising your son alone without the help of his father. If this is the case, my heart goes out to you. I realize the challenge that lies before you, but I also want to encourage you that your son can overcome the odds with the help of the Lord.

My parents divorced when I was five years old. At the age of five, I had no idea what divorce meant. I didn't realize that my father wouldn't be there to tell me about my heritage, nor would he be there to prophesy my future. He would exit my life for years. (We did not have a connection until I had become an adult.)

My mother remarried and her new husband didn't like me. There was always a rub between us. I wasn't drawn to him in any way as a replacement of my father. We coexisted in the same home, but there was not one ounce of mutual respect between us.

There was something deep within me that spoke to my inner thoughts, like an echo that would reinforce my character saying, *"Life doesn't have to be this way. One day, you will marry and treat your wife the way that you want your mother to be treated. You will raise your children the way you wanted to be raised."*

As simple as that sounds, it was that motivational inner speech that encouraged me during difficult days, weeks, months, and years.

Years later, I married my beautiful wife, Kay. We had three wonderful children. When I tucked my children into bed, my habit was to make up a story about a child who needed faith in order to get through a tough situation, and then I would pray for them, saying, *"God, I thank you that my son is strong in the Lord and mighty in his faith. Tonight, we sleep in peace, and tomorrow we will awaken in confidence, able to face the day, in Jesus' Name."*

One night after tucking my son into bed, I was walking down the stairs and spoke a desperate plea, *"God, I have never been tucked into bed."*

Suddenly, I felt has if I were five years old again. I felt the emotional pain of my father's absence. I felt the sting of my parent's divorce. I suddenly became overwhelmed with depression. It was crushing to my spirit.

The next day, during my prayer time, I sat down without saying a word. I sat there for what seemed to be an hour. Then a whisper resonated within me. I sensed the voice of God speaking to me, saying to the deepest part of my heart, *"I have given you the spirit of my Son, so that you can call me 'Daddy.' I am with you. I will never abandon you. I will not leave you as an orphan. Call me 'Father'—yes, even 'Daddy.' And I will tuck you in each night."*

That day, a work of healing took place in my spirit that allowed me to forgive on a level that was more than just a human decision. It was a spiritual act of grace. It allowed me to spew out the bitter morsels that had haunted me for years.

Father to the fatherless, defender of widows—this is
God, whose dwelling is holy.

Psalm 68:5 NLT

Knowing God as my Father, not only repaired the deep wound in
my spirit but it also allowed me to focus on my future as a father.
The change was so profound that it transformed my language. I
began to refer to God, not in a generic term but in the personal
relational term, as "Father."

WHOM SHOULD YOUR SON CALL "DADDY"?

For years, I have struggled with something that simply didn't set
well whenever I heard it. I often felt nauseated when I would
hear some man say, *"I just love hurting and troubled young men.*
I invest in them, and they look to me as their father."

These kinds of statements troubled me. I couldn't put my finger
on it until I read what Jesus said in Matthew 23:9. *"And call no*
man your father upon the earth: for one is your Father, which is in
heaven."

Obviously, I am not making a blanket statement about every
man, but I am concerned by the motives of those who draw
vulnerable young men around themselves and take the position
of "daddy." Sometimes these relationships are perverted. Any
relationship with another man who is not your son's biological
father should be carefully monitored.

Please don't think that I am calling into question the motives of
all men who are compassionate to help troubled teens. But if
you are a single parent, please be very careful whom you allow
to have influence in your son's life.

I highly recommend that you do not allow your son to call any man "father," unless he is your son's biological father. I know that people will disagree with me on this point, but I have seen too many circumstances of perverted men who have taken advantage of troubled boys.

Again, please understand what I'm saying. Not every man who takes on the role of a mentor is perverted. The Apostle Paul referred to having sons in the faith, especially Timothy, who was very dear and close to him; however, calling a man, "daddy," is a very familiar term and it should be reserved for a child's biological father.

STEPFATHERS

Let me say a word about stepfathers regarding this rule of thumb. Obviously, there are a lot of blended families today, and stepfathers play an incredible role in raising children.

As I have mentioned before, my mother remarried after she and my father divorced. Her second husband was not much of a stepfather to me, so I never called him "father" or "dad." I didn't refer to him in any parental capacity. He was my mother's second husband but he never officially became my stepfather. He didn't adopt me. He didn't exercise any fatherly position over me; however, he did make my life very difficult.

I know of many second husbands who have fully adopted or have extended their leadership to their wives' children from previous relationships. I find that admirable.

Biblically, the example of excellent fatherly leadership is illustrated in Joseph, the husband of Mary, the mother of Jesus.

Joseph could have dismissed Mary from his life and voided his pledge to marry her, but hearing directly from the angel of the Lord, Joseph chose to treat Mary with special respect and attention regarding her pregnancy. The Bible is very clear that Joseph was a man of faith. He treated Jesus with the utmost respect as his stepson.

Joseph was so in tune with the Holy Spirit that he received promptings and warnings regarding the safety of his family. He took his family to Egypt to escape Herod's wrath and saved young Jesus from destruction (Matthew 2:13-20).

We don't have any biblical record of Joseph's death. He is noticeably absent in the story after Jesus' youth; however, from all indications, Joseph was an honorable husband and father.

If a man takes on the full role and position of becoming a child's father, by marriage to his mother and especially by full adoption of that child, I believe he could be called "father" or "dad" or "daddy." I believe that this should be the child's decision.

GIVE YOUR SON DIRECTIONAL INTENT

> *Direct your children onto the right path, and when they are older, they will not leave it.*
> *Proverbs 22:6 NLT*

Your son must have directional intent in his life concerning his relationships. If you allow your son to wander through his teenage years without learning about and discovering purposeful and meaningful relationships with girls, he will not know how to navigate the challenges of hormonal change. He may be confused by the changes in his body and his personal desires, if you do not give him advanced knowledge of what to expect.

Samson is a great example of a gifted young man—physically strong, and even anointed by God for a great purpose in life—yet he was amazingly weak willed in his relationships. Samson is famous for his brilliant riddles but he is also notorious for being deceived by a woman.

From birth, Samson had directional intent in many regards. His parents imposed upon him the vow of a Nazarite. His commitment included abstaining from alcohol, refraining from his hair being cut, and not being defiled by touching a corpse. For many years he kept this vow, yet he was undisciplined in the rest of his affairs. As dedicated as he was in his vow, his parents did not direct his intentions toward marriage. Samson was fatally attracted to the wrong kind of women.

I know you want the best for your son regarding his relationships with women. You must intentionally guide him into finding the right woman. You will want to have early talks with him and often, reminding him of how important it is to be selective of whom he dates and chooses to be his wife.

This can be reinforced and helped greatly if you and he have the active support of your local church.

Here are eight keys to give your son directional intent in his relationships with the opposite sex:

1. **Don't expect your son to learn about sexuality on his own.** Talk to him directly and look for good resources that he can read.

2. **Don't rely upon public education to be the source for morality.** You must set the standard of sexual morality. Public education is far too liberal and is often misguided when it comes to sexual education.
3. **God made men and women with perfectly complimentary designs.** Purpose is fulfilled by function; therefore, the original intent for man is to find a wife for procreation.
4. **Sex is the act of blood covenant that consummates a marriage.** Sex is a sacred rite and should be reserved only for the faithfulness of a spouse.
5. **Only the male has life-giving seed.** A man must protect his progeny to be deposited within a worthy woman.
6. **The body is not meant for immorality.** Sexual immorality degrades the human body. It literally sows seeds of destruction in the body's physiology.
7. **Sex is designed to express love, not to create love.**
8. **Teach your son to distinguish between the true attraction of a woman and the lure of romanticism.**

DISCIPLESHIP AND DISCIPLINE

Discipline your son, for in that there is hope; do not be a willing party to his death.

Proverbs 19:18 NIV

Without discipline you are willingly surrendering your child to outside forces to control his behavior.

When you fail to discipline your child you are surrendering him to the correction of society. That's a harsh reality, because the world's system doesn't act out of mercy. Their primary motivation is strictly justice.

Here are some lessons I've learned as a parent to help me instruct my son:

1. **You must stay in control of your own emotions in order to guide the emotions of your child.** Some parents don't discipline until they've reached a boiling point. When they've "had enough," they burst into an uncontrollable rage. Don't do that. Calmly approach discipline. The very purpose of discipline is to teach your son to control his emotions and appetites. If you can't demonstrate control, the lesson will be lost.

2. **The purpose of discipline is to change inappropriate behavior and to give your child the ability to discern between right and wrong.** Be very specific as to why you are disciplining your children. They must know what it is that they did wrong.

3. **Establish discipline early in life, so you won't have to use it as much later.** To do this, make sure that you watch over your words and perform them. If your children do not have confidence in your discipline, they will not trust in your promises either.

4. **Don't count to three.** Parents have a ridiculous habit of counting to three (or five or ten) before they will discipline their children. This trains a child to think he can delay obedience. Teach your child to obey your words immediately. If you don't, he will transfer this understanding to his relationship with God, assuming he will always receive multiple warnings before he experiences the consequences of sin.

5. **Match the punishment to the offense.** Make certain that you don't exaggerate the punishment. Don't ground your child "for life." This will teach them that you do not watch over your words, and what you say cannot be trusted.

6. **Teach your son that it is better to live under the blessings of your hands than under the curse.** Always connect disobedience with lack, and obedience with supply. If your son is believing for something (a cell phone, clothes, a car, etc.), don't remove their daily needs, but delay their wants to discipline them.

7. **Set the tone early in life, so you won't have to deal with rebellion as he gets older.** Before he reaches rebellious actions, a child will speak disrespectfully or cuttingly toward you. If you stop him at the level of his words, you can avoid rebellion in action.

8. **Don't be intimidated by your son.** Don't let him manipulate or threaten you. Stay in control. Do NOT surrender your leadership.

GET PRACTICAL

- Teach your son to open the door for a lady.
- Teach your son not to walk through a door before a woman.
- Teach your son how to have polite dinner conversation and proper manners at the dinner table.
- Buy your son a nice suit and a pair of good dress shoes.
- Teach him how to tie a necktie.
- Purchase books for your son on how a gentleman acts. (Brooks Brothers has a selection of these titles. Brooks Brothers is classic American men's style.)
- Make sure whenever your son goes on a date, he has directional intent. He should know exactly what they will do together, where they will eat, and know how to conduct himself with dignity.
- Watch carefully who has influence over your son.
- Don't allow your son to speak in a derogatory manner to you. He will transition that kind of behavior to his girlfriend

or wife in later years.
• Read Proverbs daily.

A FivestarMan gains understanding of the deep purpose of having gallant relationships. He will passionately pursue a life of authentic manhood. He will avoid the majority of pitfalls that trip up so many men.

Chapter Four
HE NEEDS CHARACTER, NOT JUST TALENT

The man of integrity walks securely, but he who takes crooked paths will be found out.

Proverbs 10:9 NIV

The FivestarMan is faithful in his character. He is authentic in the truest sense of the word. You want your son to live up to the original intent of manhood—ethical in business, principled in relationships, and spiritual in his walk with God.

Contrary to popular belief, men are overwhelmingly spiritual; however, men are not religious. Men are practical in their faith, not pious. Men want a real relationship with God, not to join a religious sect or organization.

Earlier than you may think, your son will begin a spiritual journey. It is in the heart of man to do so. This will happen through two primary ways: *In the daily commute and in the spiritual encounter.*

A spiritual encounter often takes place in a corporate setting, such as at a church service or in a special meeting. A corporate setting is important for worship. It's primarily for the strengthening and fellowship of other believers. A strong local church will be a tremendous help to you in raising your son; however, you must know that God will also develop a personal and spiritual walk with your son.

God relates to man in the daily commute.

- Adam walked with God in the cool of the day (Genesis 3:8).
- Enoch walked with God, and he was no more for God took him (Genesis 5:24).
- Noah walked with God as a righteous man in a wicked generation (Genesis 6:9).
- Abraham walked with God to a place that he didn't know where he was going (Hebrews 11:8).
- Moses walked with God on the Holy Mountain (Exodus 19:3).
- David walked with God in the valley of the show of death (Psalm 23:4).
- Jesus, God with us, walked with His disciples, relating to them on a practical level.

If the Lord delights in a man's way, he makes his steps firm.

Psalm 37:23 NIV

When your son develops a walk with God, he will learn to discern the voice of God, and the voice of a stranger will not distract him. It is an amazing maturing process for a son who wants the advice of his Heavenly Father. This is a vital development in his relationship with God.

I noticed early on that God would quicken my spirit. I recall hearing the voice of God when I was twelve. At that age, it was almost alarming how easy it was to hear the voice of God. Even though I was naïve, young, and uneducated in the things of God, I heard the distinctive voice of God whispering in my ear about my future.

The voice of God prompted me to take certain steps. Even before I accepted Christ as my Savior, the voice of God was whispering to me. It may be more theologically correct to say it was the voice of my conscience—either way, I knew it as what was right for me. It gave me directional intent for my life.

Your son will hear God's voice. The challenge for you is not to interrupt God, but to support His direction for your son. This will require discipline on your part. Most mothers want to direct the steps of their sons; however, you must respect the personal relationship that God the Father has with your son.

Mary learned this lesson while raising Jesus. Following the Festival of Passover, Jesus' family was returning home, but He remained in the Temple in Jerusalem for three days. When his parents found Him, Jesus was teaching the teachers.

When asked what He was doing and why He had stayed, Jesus' response was telling: *"Why were you searching for me? Didn't you know I had to be in my Father's house?"* (Luke 2:49)

Interestingly enough, Jesus was twelve years of age when this occurred. It seems to be anecdotal evidence, but again, it seems there is something spiritually significant about the age of twelve for a boy. If your son is younger than twelve, you may want to be aware of it.

AN ENCOUNTER WITH GOD

Jesus gave us an outline to speak with God as our Father. This facilitates an encounter with God. This is a great way to teach your son to pray to his Heavenly Father, who waits to hear from him.

Our Father in heaven,
hallowed be your name.
Your kingdom come,
Your will be done,
on earth as it is in heaven.
Give us today our daily bread,
and forgive us our debts,
as we also have forgiven our debtors.
And lead us not into temptation,
but deliver us from the evil one.
Matthew 6:9-13 NIV

Let's break this down in detail:

Father—The word "God" is actually a generic term. I prefer to address God as Father, in the same manner that Jesus addressed Him. It is much more intimate and respectful.

Hallowed Be Your Name—Our Father is holy. This statement is an act of protocol recognizing the holiness of God the Father. Jesus instructed us to address the Father by coming to Him in the Name of Jesus.

Whatever you ask in my name, the Father will give you.
John 15:16 NIV

The Name of Jesus is like the key that unlocks the door of Heaven. In fact, it is the only key. No other name is given to men for salvation (Acts 4:12), so use the Name of Jesus to speak with the Father.

Your Kingdom Come—Teach your son to ask the Father to exercise His ways and principles in his life. When we ask the Father in faith to do His will on the earth, it gives Him a license to intervene in our world.

Asking God for His kingdom to come means that your son is inviting God to intervene in his activities and behavior with His way of doing things. It is appropriating God's way of being and doing into your son's life.

You want God's intervention in your son's life. This willing invitation will do wonders in his walk with God.

Give Us Today Our Daily Bread—This teaches your son to look to his Father God to be his Source.

There will be times that your son must look to God the Father as the Supplier of his needs. With this recognition, your son will be empowered to see his relationship with God the Father as something very personal, and the Father will look out for his success.

Forgive Us Our Sins—Teach your son that his Heavenly Father is a forgiver. God doesn't hold grudges. Your son needs to understand this incredible truth. God forgives sin.

Your son will make mistakes. He will willfully commit sin. He needs to understand that God is a God to run to, not run from, when he has failed.

*If we confess our sins, he is faithful and just to forgive us
our sins, and to cleanse us from all unrighteousness.*
                                                    1 John 1:9

Boys are prone to seek approval from their fathers. If your son
doesn't have a father approving him, you need to especially
affirm the relationship that he has with God the Father.

One word of caution here: Don't go to the extreme to suggest
that anything he does is acceptable to his Heavenly Father. No,
God is displeased with sin. Sin will have its consequences, if
your son doesn't take his relationship with God seriously. The
sacrifice of Christ was not a trivial pursuit and should not be
treated lightly.

**As We Also Have Forgiven Everyone Who Sins Against
Us**—A compassionate response to those who have sinned
against us should well up out of our gratitude that we are
forgiven. Teaching your son to respond to those who have
wronged him, hurt him in some manner, or have sinned against
him will equip him with the most powerful and divinely inspired
attribute given to men.

It also protects your son from developing a bitter root and anger
toward people. You don't want your son to become embittered.
Unforgiveness is a harsh and destructive emotional response
toward people.

**Lead Us Not Into Temptation And Deliver Us From The
Evil One**—Ask God to direct the steps of your son away from
temptation and evil.

Solomon gives this great piece of advice to his son, *"Listen, my son, to your father's instruction and do not forsake your mother's teaching"* (Proverbs 1:8 NIV).

He goes on to warn the young man about dangers of the herd mentality. Falling in with those who want to get into trouble, hurt others or rob people is deadly (Proverbs 1:10-18). It is vitally important that you warn your son not go along with the herd or the gang.

LEAD YOUR FAMILY IN FAITH

With the help of God, you must lead your family in faith.

If you're going to raise your son to be a FivestarMan, it will require you to walk with God yourself.

Don't underestimate the influence of your faith. Be consistent. Your son sees the dedication that you have toward God. He will respect you for it.

With that in mind, you must watch how you conduct yourself with other men. If you are inconsistent in your faith, you could do irreparable harm to your son's faith. If you are confessing a faith in God, yet the corresponding characteristics of faith are not evident in your life, your son will see the hypocrisy. That doesn't mean you must be perfect, but you should be authentic in your beliefs.

Teach your son to have a personal faith and relationship with God the Father through Jesus Christ.

WATCH OVER YOUR WORDS

Your words are incredibly important to your son. He must be able to believe you. He must see that you value what you say and will hold yourself accountable to do it.

Let your son overhear you praying and interceding for him. This isn't for show; it is real. Jesus did this when He prayed.

> *Father, I thank you that you have heard me. I knew that you always hear me, but I said this for the benefit of the people standing here, that they may believe that you sent me.*
>
> *John 11:41-42*

When you face challenges, invite your son to join you. Don't cower under the pressure you are facing. Be strong in raising your son. You will get through this with your faith. Let him see it, and you will strengthen him.

Hearing you pray and seeing the answers that you receive will give your son confidence to look to God the Father for himself.

LET HIM SEE YOU READING THE BIBLE

Read the Word of God for your own edification but let it spill over into your son's life. Don't quote chapter and verse at him, using it like a club. Speak kind and comforting words. Focus on the affirmations of the verses that encourage, build up and inspire.

Let the Scriptures flow from your lips like honey, paraphrasing it in your own words, so long as you don't misspeak the meaning of the passages.

*Study and be eager and do your utmost to present
yourself to God approved (tested by trial), a workman
who has no cause to be ashamed, correctly analyzing
and accurately dividing [rightly handling and skillfully
teaching] the Word of Truth.*

2 Timothy 2:15 AMP

RELATE TO YOUR SON AS A BROTHER IN CHRIST

This will give you a respectful line of appreciation for how you are raising him.

Some mothers never allow their sons to grow up and be men. You want your son to mature in his life and especially in his faith. As he grows, this will require you to allow a distance in your relationship.

Amazingly the distance of respect actually closes the proximity of the relationship. This is a difficult concept for some to grasp, but I have seen it work in all of my relationships. The relationships that flourish all have a line of mutual respect. All of the relationships that became familiar were lost in disrespect.

Mothers who do not allow their sons to create a distance end up losing their sons' presence in their lives altogether.

With that in mind, let me share a few keys to governing relationships. Teach your son these lessons:

- Don't trust someone who doesn't respect your relationship

with God (Psalm 14:1).
- Don't trust someone who mocks God (Proverbs 19:3).
- Don't trust someone who creates his own religion. Some men design their own belief systems to fit their lifestyles (Proverbs 28:26).
- Don't trust someone who is always in contention with another person (Proverbs 18:6).
- Don't trust someone who continues to repeat the same mistakes over and over (Proverbs 26:11).
- Don't trust someone who bursts out in tantrums and rages to get his way (Proverbs 27:3).
- Never underestimate the destructive power of simple-minded men (Proverbs 24:9).

CHARACTER QUALITIES TO DEVELOP IN YOUR SON

I am convinced God has placed a deposit of ability, skill and talent within each of us. That means your son has a special skill set. If he learns how to draw upon these skills while building up his character, it will give him an unlimited future.

Teach him the difference between dreams and schemes. A dream is a worthy goal; a scheme is a fantasy. Don't allow your son to chase fantasies on the path to developing the abilities and talents that are within him.

Remember that talent will only take your son so far. The true mark of a man is his character.

Here are twelve very important character traits your son will need to develop in order to be the authentic man God has called him to be.

1. CLARITY OF VISION

Teach your son the importance of minding the details while having a long-range goal. Understand that long range for your son will not necessarily be ten years down the road. Long range for him may be a few months or, possibly, a couple of years, but it is imperative that he develops an eye for the details while focusing on fulfilling a dream.

This character trait will help your son delay his desire for instant gratification and give him an advantage over his peers.

2. THE ABILITY TO SPEAK CLEARLY

Teach your son to be articulate and value what he says. The Apostle Paul said, "Pray that I may speak clearly as I should; making the most of the opportunity" (Ephesians 6:20; 5:16).

I have especially noticed a lack of confidence in young men who did not have the influence of a father when they were growing up. This insecurity is often revealed when speaking to other men. They may fail to make eye contact and speak clearly.

As a young man, I struggled with this lack for a couple of reasons: (1) I had a speech impediment as a boy that took countless hours of therapy to get over; and (2) I simply didn't know how to speak to another person with confidence.

Teach your son to stand up straight with his shoulders back, to make eye contact, and to articulate accurate and appropriate words when speaking to others. And do not allow him to use expletives. Cursing is a sure sign of disrespect and ignorance. Those who use obscenities are simply empty-headed and rude.

You should also spend time developing your son's vocabulary to help build his confidence. Knowing what to say and when to say it will give him the ability to open up to you and to others.

3. CLEAN HANDS

I know, you're probably still getting over the chapter on "Raising A Dirty Boy," but in this case, I mean that it is important to teach your son to do business with integrity.

Business integrity is an absolute must in protecting your son's potential. Teach him the value of a contract and a handshake. Make sure that he knows his words are his bond. He must fulfill his promises.

4. THE RECOGNITION AND AVOIDANCE OF EVIL

Bored young men tend to gravitate toward stupidity. If they are not active, their undeveloped brains will devise all kinds of schemes. If you're going to protect your son from evil, keep him actively pursuing worthy goals and causes. Keep him busy.

5. THE CONTROL OF HIS TONGUE

It is imperative that your son learns that the tongue is destructive and can damage others. The harm done by the tongue can be irreparable.

Teach your son not to wrong another person with his speech by reminding him that he should not use embarrassing nicknames for people or bully weaker people with his mouth. Teach him never to position himself above another person intellectually—not to think of himself as mentally superior to others or try to show that he is.

6. THE WISDOM NOT TO TAKE OFFENSE

Although your son will learn the valuable lesson of not misusing his tongue to hurt people, others will use their tongues to try to hurt him. There will always be people who are jealous and envious of him. Teach him to accept the envy as a compliment, rather than an insult.

Proverbs teaches, *"Overlook an offense, and cement a friendship"* (Proverbs 17:9 Author's paraphrase). The rare ability to overlook an offense will separate your son from the crowd of emotionally weak people. This is truly one of the greatest life skills that a young man can develop. Once your son accepts the fact that not everyone will approve of him, he will have the ability to make personal decisions rather than attempt to please others for approval.

7. PRUDENCE

You don't hear much about prudence, but it is an art form. If your son is prudent, he will take care of his possessions. Solomon said, *"He who gathers crops in summer is a prudent son, but he who sleeps during harvest is a disgraceful son"* (Proverbs 10:5 NIV).

Teach your son to be responsible and to take care of his possessions. It truly is a character quality that will pay a huge return in his life.

- Teach him to make his bed. No one else is responsible to make his bed in life. This simple lesson teaches personal responsibility.
- Teach him to keep his bike or his car clean. Properly caring for a car keeps it running well and maintained. It will save you both a lot of money. I recommend that whenever you fill up with gas, the car should be cleaned, as well. (This is

simply a part of a routine maintenance plan for me.)
- Teach him to read the instruction manuals for the things that he owns.
- Teach him to take proper care of his clothes, fold them and put them away. (You may want to show him what should be dry-cleaned.)

8. SELF-DISCIPLINE

One of the greatest foes of authentic manhood is a man's appetite.

Noah was a great man, a discerning man who foresaw calamity coming upon the world and built an ark to save his family; yet, after the danger had passed, he planted a vineyard and drank too much wine. One night of drunkenness exposed his son to a generational curse.

Teaching your son to stay in control of his personal appetites will be a key to him living a long and prosperous life. Make sure that he has healthy eating habits and an exercise routine.

9. THE UNDERSTANDING OF MONEY

We've talked about this in the chapter entitled, "Make Your Son A Money Magnet"; however, this is worth revisiting briefly. Money is simply a means to an end. It is a tool in the hands of a skilled craftsman. Teach your son how to use money to advance his purpose, not to just temporarily satisfy his cravings.

10. DILIGENCE

Honestly, this is a game changer. Teaching your son to be diligent will be the difference maker in his life. His success will be directly related to this single character trait.

To be diligent means to work hard, to be attentive to the details, and to be busy, constant and persistent in devotion to what he is doing. This kind of focus is the kind of work that gets attention. Promotion will be a regular occurrence in your son's life if you teach him diligence.

- Diligent hands bring wealth (Proverbs 10:4).
- Diligent hands rule (Proverbs 12:24).
- The desires of the diligent are fully satisfied (Proverbs 13:4).
- Diligence leads to profit (Proverbs 21:5).
- Being diligent will give you progress (1 Timothy 4:15).

11. A LOVE OF LEARNING

Do not allow your son to buy into the idea that men are simpletons and are not readers. Develop your son's appetite for reading. You can do this by reading to him when he is young. You can cultivate this appetite in his youth by continually supplying him with reading material.

There were books that I read as a young man that are still impacting my life today. For an example, I realized when I was seventeen that I needed wisdom. I picked up a book entitled, **See You At The Top,** by Zig Ziglar. In it, Mr. Ziglar encouraged me to read one chapter of Proverbs every day of the month. That one recommendation has had more impact on my life than I can measure. Since then I have read hundreds of books; yet, few have had the impact that Zig's book had on my impressionable youth.

12. TEACH YOUR SON TO BUILD HIS LIFE ON THE WORD OF GOD

- Reading the Word of God is the energy of life (John 1:4).
- Reading the Word of God renews the mind and keeps it clear of offense (Psalm 119:165).
- Reading the Word of God scrubs off stinking thinking (John 15:3).
- Reading the Word of God will protect your son from impurity (Psalm 119:9).
- Reading the Word of God instructs him in righteousness (2 Timothy 3:16).
- Reading the Word of God will promote your son above his competition (Psalm 119:98).
- Reading the Word of God will illuminate his spirit (Psalm 119:130).
- Reading the Word of God will help make your son happy (John 15:11).
- Reading the Word of God clearly identifies right from wrong (Proverbs 3:7).
- Reading the Word of God will give your son wisdom (Proverbs 2:6).

GET PRACTICAL

- Teach your son to commune with God as he is going to school. If you drive him to school, spend some time praying about the day. Express praise to God for the day, his teachers, the administrators and the opportunity to learn.
- Inspect what you expect. If you expect him to make his bed, go into his room and hold him accountable to do it.
- Make sure that he picks up after himself. You're not his maid.
- Hold him accountable for the money that he receives from

you. Know what he spends it on and make sure that he
tells you the truth.
- Make sure that he is diligent—remember, this is the
  character trait that makes or breaks his success in life.
- Make sure that you purchase books for him to read,
  especially biographies on great men.
- Have him go to www.fivestarman.com and read the
  "Daily Champion," a daily encouragement that will link to
  Proverbs which correspond with each day of the month.
  Developing this habit now will be a life changer for him.

When your son is raised with the characteristics of authentic
manhood, he will want to design and live a life that matters. A
FivestarMan is a man who is faithful in his character.

This will lead him to his next purpose of living for a cause and
leaving a legacy.

Chapter Five
HE HAS A CAUSE WORTH FIGHTING FOR

A young mother of two children, both with behavioral challenges, in the midst of a divorce, took her boys to a local Pizza Hut. Even though her six-year old son's Asperger's syndrome and ADHD medication had worn off, she worked to maintain social decorum and keep her children entertained.

Sitting across from her in a booth nearby, a man politely acknowledged her efforts with a nod and left the restaurant.

Soon after, a teary-eyed waitress handed a note to the struggling mother. It read:

> "I do not know your back story, but I have had the privilege of watching you parent your children for the past 30 minutes. I have to say thank you for parenting your children in such a loving manner.
>
> I have watched you teach your children about the importance of respect, education, proper manners, communication, self-control, and kindness all while being very patient. I will never cross your path again

but I am positive that you and your children have amazing futures.

Keep up the good work, and when it starts to get tough do not forget that others may be watching and will need the encouragement of seeing a good family being raised. God bless! —Jake"

This simple gesture encouraged the young mother with the idea that the man must have been an angel, or at least he had been used of God to send her such an encouraging note.

A CAUSE WORTH FIGHTING FOR

I can't imagine the struggle that you may be facing as a mother, but I want to encourage you. The fact that you are reading this book already testifies that you have a cause worth fighting for: the raising of your son.

"Is there not a cause?" —King David

Your son wants a cause worthy of a fight. A FivestarMan is philanthropic in his nature. He wants to make a difference in the world.

If your son doesn't have a cause worth fighting for he will find the wrong thing to fight against.

We're seeing a generation of young people who really don't have anything to fight for. Confused by the empty rhetoric of false causes, they rally on Wall Street against an unknown identity, the top 1%. They have food, clothing, elite-educations, all the while holding their Starbucks cinnamon dolcé lattes, but they're angry enough to sleep in the parks for their cause, no matter how silly and underserving of a cause it may be.

This is not the kind of cause that you want to raise your son to fight for. It's not worthy of him.

You should remember that you are preparing your son for his mission. I know that's a pretty heavy statement, but it's true. You're not just raising an executive, or an athlete, or a professional salesman, you're raising a man on a mission.

Your goal is not to raise a good boy into a good man. You are assigned the responsibility to raise a boy who has a deep reservoir of purpose within him. That purpose is a philanthropic cause.

> ...God has also set eternity in the hearts of men.
> Ecclesiastes 3:11 NIV

Every man has a deep desire to do something of significance. To live beyond one's self is the desire of authentic man. The word "philanthropic" means "the active effort to better humanity; to use one's gifts, talents, resources, and influence to create change in the lives of less fortunate people."

When you draw upon this deep passion within your son, you will discover that his purpose to live for the sake of others taps into a creativity and spiritual consciousness that will not be revealed in any other way.

Tapping into this depth of purpose will truly distinguish your son from the crowd. Few men ever get to this level of understanding. Most men are too busy living for themselves or being tripped up in the silly little snares of sophomoric pursuits.

If you want your son to experience the highest level of pure joy and satisfaction in life, train your son to live for a cause. Elevate his pursuits above cars, clothes and cottages. Lift him up to the desire to fight for a cause.

A FivestarMan understands that he uses his entrepreneurial drive to gain the resources, influence and finances in his life to meet his needs, to provide for his family and to leave them an inheritance, but he has also accumulated enough to leave the world a better place because he has lived.

Teach your son to be observant of the needs of others. He will not be able to meet every need, but he can find something he can do. He will see a need and meet it.

This is how men are motivated. Boys have a natural tendency to be heroes. They identify with Batman, Superman, Ironman, etc., because the hero sacrificially fights for a cause.

Your son wants to be the hero. He doesn't have super powers, but he does have an incredible God-given purpose within him. That purpose will move him to action. It will motivate him to do something greater than himself.

My favorite man-movie is **Braveheart.** I am deeply moved when William Wallace says, "Aye, fight and ye may die. Run and you'll live, at least for a while. And dying in your beds many years from now, would you be willing to trade all the days from this day to that for one chance, just one chance to come back here and tell our enemies that they may take our lives, but they'll never take... our freedom!"

It is a cowardly generation who will not fight the foe that will one day enslave their children.

You want your son to fight for a cause, but that cause should be worthy of him.

TEACH YOUR SON TO LIVE WHILE HE IS LIVING

We sat down on the swing in the manicured back yard, near the shop where he refinished furniture and crafted his woodwork, a hobby that was a welcome retreat from the daily grind of his occupation. Next to the shop was a garage with his prized bass boat. He had worked the grueling labor of shift work his whole life. My father-in-law sat down and talked to me man to man, in a way he never had before.

I was no longer the naïve young man who married his daughter. I was a man who was managing my own household and building my career. He was dying. Cancer had robbed him of his hair and reduced his thick body to a slim, sickly frame.

He looked across the yard, pondering his life. He spoke softly, "Neil, live while you are living." He paused and then sighed out his regret, "I've worked all my life to retire. Now that I can, I am dying.... What a waste."

I changed my thinking that day. I decided that I would go for it—live the adventure, not just coast through the ranks. I decided that I would believe God for bigger things. It motivated me to step out and risk it all—to pursue life at a new level. Yes, I made some challenging decisions, doing things that were outside of the mainstream of thought. Yet, because of this conversation with a dying man, I realized that I wanted to embrace life and its adventure of living for a cause.

Don't allow your son to believe the lie. Don't allow your son to pattern his life after the herd, to simply go with the flow. Don't relinquish your son to a life of petty comfort. His life is more valuable than to work and labor for nothing but vanity.

It is tempting to scheme and strategize a career path for your son. Don't do it. Don't put limits on him. God may have something incredible, significant and admirable for your son to accomplish.

Don't motivate your son to chase the fleeting illusion of fame. An authentic man wants significance. He wants his brief time on this earth to matter.

Your son was born for significance. He was uniquely gifted, not only to make a living, not only to impact your family, but also to change the world in some way.

I believe that.

You will need to select a church that supports and undergirds the ideas of authentic manhood. Modern Christianity has replaced the adventurous, global impacting, risk taking, sacrificial faith of Christ and converted it into a weak, anemic, pacifist, tolerant, religion of appeasement. That kind of religion doesn't understand Jesus' statement, *"The Kingdom of Heaven forcefully advances"* (Matthew 11:12 NLT).

Your son will need to be nurtured by men who take action in life, not just talk about it. Too many churches are all talk and no action.

The eleventh chapter of Hebrews is often called the "Hall of Faith." Those listed in this exclusive club did remarkable things that could not be accomplished without an active faith in God and a belief that they were personally selected by God to impact their world in their time.

You may conclude that it requires faith to believe in creation. It may for some. I believe the evidence overwhelmingly supports that the universe is not an accident, where some "bang" simply happened. I believe that God said, "Let there be light," and, "bang," it was so.

If you look closely at Hebrews 11:3, you'll see something interesting that will help you motivate your son toward significance. What were those historical figures, who impacted their time and are still being talked about, commended or credited for?

They were credited for what it says in that verse.

> By faith we understand that the universe was formed at God's command, so that what is seen was not made out of what was visible.
>
> Hebrews 11:3 NIV

Now let's break that down into its literal meaning from the Greek language: The word "universe" is "zion" in the Greek, which means "generation." The word "formed" means "to change, to shape, to fashion, or to mold." The phrase "God's command" means "speaking revelation."

Here's the point. The list of those mentioned in the "Hall of Faith," were commended for "exercising faith by speaking revelation that molded their generations."

Apply that to your son. Is it possible that if your son believes God for significance he could change or mold his generation?

Why not?

I have seen remarkable things happen in the lives of ordinary men. I've seen boys come up out of the worst of situations and be recognized as world changers.

GET PRACTICAL

- Find an opportunity for your son to do meaningful charity work.
- If your mother or father needs some work done around the house, have your son do it for them. Helping his grandparents provides a great lesson in respect for the elderly. If they are not nearby, have him help a neighboring widow.
- Have him clean his closet once a year to give some of his clothes to a charity. Make sure that he is the one who sorts and folds the clothes for the gift. This will provide him with a great lesson on gratitude.
- If he mows lawns for summer work, have him mow a widow's lawn for free. This will teach him to give to those who are in need.
- When he is a young man, have him go on a missions trip with your church. Seeing the needs of others contrasted with the lifestyle of American privilege will make him more grateful for his blessings.
- Teach him to give the first ten percent of his income to the Church as a Tithe of his income. This biblical practice will position your son to win in life and rule over his own money.

Regardless of the circumstances that have impacted your life, the challenges of raising your son and the trials of our times, could it be that you are raising a boy on a mission, with a cause worthy of this fight?

I believe so.

You are raising a FivestarMan.

CONCLUSION

I want to conclude this book with a word of hope.

God has a great plan for your son. The circumstances that you are facing in raising him may not be perfect, but God is wonderfully equipped to overcome the shortcomings of our lives and grace us for our tasks.

My prayer for you is that you will come to understand that over the next few years, your son will grow into a man—an authentic man. As he is growing stronger, you will marvel at the changes that come about in him. He will distinguish himself and walk in the dignity of manhood. This culture will not define him. God will not abandon you or your son. God will help you. Our Heavenly Father will father your son.

Don't give up.

Don't become weary in well doing.

Don't allow the enemy to deceive you. What you're doing is an incredible endeavor, and God will help you.

One day, your son will walk out the door with his arms around his wife, maybe with his children clinging to his legs. You will watch him drive away. It will be a bittersweet moment. Your son will have grown to be a man with his own family. And as he goes, you will know that you raised a FivestarMan.

God bless you.

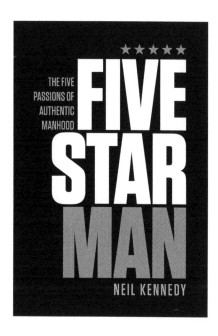

In **Fivestarman–The Five Passions Of Authentic Manhood,** Neil Kennedy digs deep into the five passions of authentic manhood. When God created Man, he placed within him a deep reservoir of purpose. Flowing within that reservoir is a commodity worth more than gold. It truly is the currency of your life. If you can gain understanding of it, you will never again be concerned about the subsistence level of living–clothes, cars, and cottages. You will be able to focus on what really matters–which is the purpose of your existence as an authentic man.

Description: 6" x 9"; Paperback; 182 pages.

The **Fivestarman Field Guide and 45-Day Challenge** is your opportunity to embrace and process the Five Passions of Authentic Manhood into your life. Over the next 45 days you will draw upon deep rivers of authentic manhood and awaken passions that reside within you. Make no mistake – this isn't a program to make you something that you are not but rather to reveal the original intent of what God made you to be.

The purpose of the handy, pocket-sized printed guide is to allow you to carry it with you everywhere you go throughout the day so that you can refer to each day's challenge and keep yourself on track.

Description: 4" x 6"; Paperback; 90 pages

These and other resources available at
fivestarman.com